Lyrical Dismay

Lyrical Dismay

Or

'The After Effects of a Brainfart'

Seth Jones

To order additional copies of this book, contact:
Xlibris Corporation
0-800-644-6988
www.xlibrispublishing.co.uk
Orders@Xlibrispublishing.co.uk
301128

Contents

The Anger

Acceptance

Moving On

3 years on

This collection is dedicated to
Everyone who has ever influenced or touched my life.
Especially my boys for giving me courage.
And to all the survivors out there.
You are never alone!

Introduction

This book follows the break up of my marriage in poetry.
I released all my anger and frustration through these words.
I hope you enjoy the read and will not label this work as a
load of rubbish, which it probably is.

The Break Up

Abandoned

We are not loved enough
Left behind in this charade
This existence is so rough
I struggle to keep my head up
Forever being pushed down
By this feeling of inadequacy
Made to feel like a clown
A coward, A foolish child

We who are left behind
Struggle to survive
Bereft of a love so kind
We fight a battle in our heads
Existing only for pain
We hide from ourselves
With nothing to gain
We are abandoned

Absolution

I am forever seeking
That which I cannot find
My mind is in turmoil
I am stuck in a bind
Things that I said
Things that I have done
Leave much to be desired
Of hope, I have none
All this crazy insanity
This complete madness revealed
Brings me to my knees
Praying my fate is not sealed
But still I look around
Hoping for a revelation
I have not found it yet
My prayer, my absolution

Betrayed

I am wounded
Nigh unto death
My heart is bleeding
And my head is a mess

Conflicting emotions
Rule my life
Caring for nothing
My lot, toil and strife

In this wakened nightmare
Strange emotions gather
Coiling like snakes
Slithering in my brain

Oh when will it end
This journey horrendous
Stupefied, I stumble on
Hoping for whatever outcome may be

Brainstorm

Why can I not see
What is in front of me?
Chasing all my hopes and dreams away
I live in madness another day

Wishing always for death
That peaceful sleep
At the thought of my suffering
I break down and weep

Brainstorm
Confused thoughts
Driven to obscurity
Obsessive purity

I am so lost
Doomed to pay the cost
A lifetime of regret
My way and mind are set

Not knowing that I can change
Wandering in tunnel vision
Trying to escape my mind
separating myself with incision

This is my brainstorm
My voice lost in the wind
Howling in my mind
Myself I will never find

Howling wind of obscurity
Lightning flash of pain
Thunderclap of ignorance
pushing me down again

Malcontent forces
Seeking me to control
Cowering before its power
I dig deeper in the hole

Brainstorm
A voice lost in the wind
Driven into obscurity
My obsessive purity

Break Up

I met a girl and she was great
All the things we did and ate
Makes no sense to me now
You see we have had a row

I feel so lost and alone
All I do is bitch and moan
Why don't she love me
Is my desperate constant plea

Maybe one day I'll be alright
The site of her won't give me fright
Until then I am desolate
Which is a lot better than hate

Broken

Devoid of happiness I suffer alone
In this nightmare I am on my own
A hellhole of miserable madness
An eternity of incurable sadness
Try as I might, I cannot get through
My souls sad devotion to you
Lost and replaced, taken for granted
My broken heart is always enchanted
A slave to my daily misery
I am nothing, I am me
The insane thoughts in my head
Tell me that I would be better dead
I am madness, I am pain
In this life I have nothing to gain

Confusion Reigns

Confusion reigns
This is nothing new
Life's joys and pains
Mixed with thoughts of you

Madness or sorrow
Comfort or pain
An agonizing despair, the thought
that I might never be with you again

Take comfort dear heart
I am with you to the end
Though the road is hard and wearisome
I am ever your friend

Time heals all things
as it should
But some things take longer to heal
I would make it right if I could

I beg of you
Please give me the time and space
To clear my head and rest my brain
So that I may find our special place

Cranial Turbulence

The thoughts in my head
Won't leave me alone
Maybe I should be dead
Mangled flesh and broken bone
Thoughts of death
Plague my wakened hours
My last feeble breathe
Poisoning the flowers

I don't deserve an explanation
For this pain inflicted
Doomed to damnation
Mind body soul wicked
My body is lethargic
My brain is numb
Your heart so arctic
I am so dumb

Dark thoughts

The dark clouds roll in over the hills
Laden with uncried tears of grief and despair
Only a mind that is blank and empty
Could withstand this bleakness without care

For this, I was not prepared
This storm washing over me
Someone to stem the tide
Not for me, I cannot see

No more the warm fires of hearth and home
Only cold and desolate darkness
No light to guide or comfort me
This chaos, turning my mind to mess

In this dark place, forever I see
Memories of what used to be
Pictures of another life, another time
Such is the path of destiny

Mayhap in time to come
Will I see the warm light
As for now, in darkness I stand
And wait, for the cloud across my sight

To be lifted, to set me free
Free to become what I was meant to be
A being of love and forgiveness
What I once was, a man like me

Dismissed

The arrogant voice
Coldly dismissed me
I was left to myself
without any sanctity

Rejected curses
Plague my inner self
Left to die alone
Forgotten on the shelf

In this absent silence
I sit and ponder
To be part of something
Thus do I wonder

Helpless

Lost, but not alone
Together, but apart
Divided we stand
Empty space between us

My darling, I am hurt
More than words can say
These words do not fully tell you
What I really feel today

These are but words
Thoughts on paper
Expressions of emotions
Too hurtful to say

I am helpless against you
Your slave forever
But do not cry for me
When my mortal agony is over

Replace me if you like
Shout scream and curse
But I am yours forever
Whether you want me or not

It Hurts

I am suffocation
Breathing alone
So much to say
Sharp words to hone

Blatant rejection
Crushed and broken
Cancerous thoughts
Need to be spoken

This is denial
A love scorned
Broken hearted
Our union is mourned

In emotional chaos
Mind torn apart
Left in agony
With no heart

Weeping tears
Unending flows
So very sad
And no-one knows

Lost

I found the lady of my dreams
She became my nightmare
I am a stranger in my house
Barely able to breathe the air

I am mental disarray
I am emotional decay
Battered in life
Scarred for death

In my screams I hear clarity
The voice inside leading me on
All is lost and laid to waste
This love and life a proven con

I have a faulty brain
I have a dead heart
Bleeding in life
Rotting in death

There is no way out for me
Commitments were made
I never want to break them
My passions break and fade

I am nothing
I am scum
I am misery
I am undone

Loves Hate

Agony Pain
Destroyed again
Confused Lost
I cannot pay the cost
Depressed Dejected
I am rejected

Mentally deficient
I am broken
Life in pieces
Broken
Broken

Cracked Insane
Cannot escape the pain
Unloved Alone
For sins I atone
Unsure Scarred
Lessons learned hard

Mentally deficient
I am broken
Life in pieces
Broken
Broken

I love to hate
I hate to love
Broken

Loves Last Scent

Devastating darkness
Enfolding me in its morbid embrace
Lost to myself
Cold glistening tears on my face

Her light is gone
I am lost
Loves last scent
Dispersed by reality

Anguished terror
Pierces deep into my breast
Malicious madness
Not strong enough to face the rest

Insipid whispers
Lulled me to deadly sleep
Obscure caresses
Tore me open and sunk me deep

Faithless promises
Lifted and carried my sanity
Absolute endings
Lead to pain and sad infinity

Pieces

Shattered thoughts
Broken dreams
I am nothing

Torn heart
Savaged soul
I am nothing

Look at these pieces
Sweep them under the carpet
Put them out of sight
If you can't see, you can't fret

I am nothing
Broken and discarded
Cracks in my brain
Like a shattered windowpane

Nervous wreck
Emotional mess
I am nothing

Shaking body
Shivering soul
I am nothing

Questions To Myself

How can I fix this
When some else broke it
Why does my hand hurt
When I am sure the glove does fit
What is this bad dream
That plagues me in sunlight
If it is not worth it
Then why do I fight
I cannot seem to let go
It would just feel wrong
Why is my heart sad
When I should be filled with song
Struggling with the confusion
I rant and rave
Feeling grievously sore and weak
When I should be brave
My house is no more home
I cannot seem to fit in
There is no peace and quiet
When my head is filled with this din

Selfishness

In times of trouble
Make mine a double
In times of need
Forget my greed
In times of pain
I have nothing to gain

Yes I am but a man
I am someone who can
At this life I am sometimes failing
When for others it is plain sailing
A miserable man am I
Under a blue sky

In a constant fight
Searching for what's right
A war in my mind
To myself I am not kind
It is always about me
Everything is nothing, you see

Appearing to be selfish
Is my last wish
Always looking for love
That wondrous feeling from above
Never quite making the mark
Seemingly lost in the dark

Silence

This house is filled with echoes
Of a love once celebrated
Toys and things all in rows
Happiness and laughter in the air
Memories of friendly chatter
Sparkling moments that will last
A life where nothing seemed to matter
Where love was everything
But now there is only silence
Children's laughter is no more
I have no thoughts of abstinence
In this cold empty place
How did it come to this
These quiet rooms so emotionless
With agony my family do I miss
Here in this void of silence

Sometimes

Today I feel alive
I know that I will survive
It has been very hard
I have been dealt a black card
Sometimes I want to cry
Looking for somewhere to fly
It is not the answer
All these feelings for her
Her presence I could do without
My very feelings I do doubt
Sometimes I can think clearly
Sometimes I despise her dearly

The Unknown

This path I take
Leads me to places unknown
This heart you break
Crumbles before your gaze
Time to make the decision
Before your will fades away
Time to make the incision
Cut me loose and throw me away
Not knowing is pain
I am shattered by your indifference
Not knowing is insane
I wither before your gaze

What A Mess

Of unfailing loss was I born
An ignorant slave to pain
A head case shall I be
'Til my dying day

Every breathe I take
In this fight for life
Takes me closer to my nemesis
My end is nearly in sight

And when I reach the journey's end
That place of misery and pain
I will pass on and never return
For I did not deserve the life I had.

Begging and Hope

Hot And Cold

Why are you so cold
Your passion is like ice
Chilling me to the bone
Your poor freezing heart
May one day melt
And leave you drowning
In your emotional haven

Cold you are
Wall of ice
Imprisoning your heart

Remember the old times
The fires burning in your eyes
Letting the world know
Your love proclaimed
Hot emotions radiating
Energy and vitality
I was yours and you mine

Hot you were
Wall of fire
Flames in your veins

Oh my dearest love
What went so wrong
Passion to indifference
Love into hate
Can you see a way through
Can we ever get close
Is there any hope

Cold you are
Hot you were
Wall of ice
Wall of fire
Imprisoning your heart
Flames in your veins

I Needed You

I have cried myself to sleep
Once again lost and alone
Needing words of comfort
Finding a heart of stone
Was it all worth it
This hopeless charade
All the things we said
All the vows we made

Why where you so far away
When I needed you
Why could you not have stayed
When I needed you
This did not have to end
This pain
This confusion

Time to move on now
Time to find a new life
I cannot understand her
Why do I deserve this strife
Friends and family all around
Locked in a place of despair
Struggling to survive
Fighting for air

Where are you now
When I need you
Are you happy in love
When I need you
It has all come to an end
With pain
With confusion

The Way Home

I have tried to forget
This anguish in my soul
The beating of my heart
Echoing in society's hole
Falling forever
Into the unknown fear
Lost to myself
I have not the will to hear

I hear your cries
Calling my name
Your loving caress unfelt
With tender urges you came
And took my hand
Leading me away
To places of peace
Where I always want to stay

But I must go now
Depart from this place
A heart filled with terror
Tears on my face
Back to your embrace
I must find the way
Hardship strengthens me
And long is my day

But in the end
I will see you again
We will find our utopia
Regardless of the wind and rain
This is my way home
I am nevermore alone

Winters Heart

I have a heart of red and gold
The coloured hues of coming cold

Shivering with winters spreading infection
Oh damn this numbing cold rejection

My love has been ripped away
In its place does pain hold sway

Our passion was as summer bliss
Her face, her thoughts I do miss

Lost at night filled with desolation
I was her slave in blessed emancipation

Oh how I wish to see her happy face
But here I am in a darkened place

Darling, do not turn your back on me
I am yours in body and soul completely

Save me from this wintry existence
And with the spring blossoms we will dance

The Anger

Escape

How can I escape
This cursed disgrace
Overflowing with emotions
I am out of place

Trapped in this cage
I rage in futility
Trying to forget my pain
I hide in sobriety

Is nothing sacred
In this holy vow
I am struggling
In the here and now

Hearing the distant chatter
Of words filled with betrayal
Even though I try
I am doomed to fail

This life, this love
Is now empty
Devoid of caring
rejecting me

One day it will end
How I cannot say
Need to survive
Until that far off day

Fading Passion

Lost to myself
Living in eternal sorrow
I am not really alive

Lost in pain
dreading the coming curse
I am not really dead

Your love has died
With the fading of my passion
Can you remember
The past times
Can you remember
Our midnights confession

Lost in darkness
With myself to blame
I cannot survive

Lost in you
A broken man am I
I must survive

My light has died
With the fading of my passion
Can you remember
A head filled with rhymes
Can you remember
Hearts filled with absolution

Lost to myself
Lost in pain
Lost in darkness
Lost in you

Passions fade
Dispersing away
Promises made
Once upon a day

T

I
I am man
I
I am insatiable
I
I am desire

You caught my eye
While I walked on by
You had an aura of darkness
That turned me into a mess
In the corner of my eye
You where flitting like a butterfly
I want you so bad
Terror you've never had

I
I want you
I
I need you
I
I will take you

You can run and hide
I am forever inside
In the corner of your brain
turning thoughts insane
Breathing down your neck
Emotions a complete wreck
You are nothing without me
You're mine always you see

I
I have you
I
I hurt you
I
I love you

Perfidious Touch

Innocent caress on skin
Turning into a dream
Angelic creature laden with sin
Rips your life away with a scream

The echoes of past iniquity
Catches all of us
Sucking us deeper into eternity
Losing our minds and lives

These soulless creatures
Corrupt my innocence
Violent smiles are featured
Chilling my brain

Crawling ever closer
Whispering platitudes
This dark is for her
Covering and sheltering

Simpering and slithering
She coils around me
Seemingly forgetting
The anguish in her wake

The Curse

May your hearts be forever broken
And your minds torn apart
These dark words to be spoken
Originate in my scarred heart

May your lives be filled with pain
And may nothing ever work out for you
May you know loss not gain
You are scum this is true

May all your dreams turn to dust
And may you never know the joys of sharing
May your senses never adjust
To the eternal loss of caring

May all my bad wishes never come true
And may you oneday realise
That your friends are now few
That there is no waiting pleasant surprise

May you hear me now
And may you listen well
Before I take this final bow
Your soul will rot in hell

Times Gone

All I wanted was a place in your life
A little corner of your heart
Something to share with you
Your persona a work of art
This my dream of fantasy
Sustained me in my misery
Kept me from insane places
The light in my obscurity

The times we had
My heart was glad
Wanting it never to end
My lover my friend

Now all I have is confusion
A mind in constant decay
Tortured soul gone unstable
Lost to the light of day
My fantasy destroyed callously
Left to my own devices
I begin to scar and warp
Left with dangerous vices

The times we had
My heart was glad
It is all at an end
My dear anti-friend

Desolated landscape of emotion
In this place I run free
My time has gone

Unleash It

Unleash the anger
Let it flow from your body
Make it a stranger
Nevermore welcome here

Let it be my dying wish
To leave this thing behind
And find my niche
The little corner of home

I am suffering inside
This pain is tearing me open
I want to run and hide
From my bitter self

Unleash it
Into the wind
Unleash it
Into the void

Unleash your pain
Let it escape your mind
Cleanse your brain
Free of the stains

This thing you cannot see
Eating you up inside
It is the enemy
Behind friendly lines

Forget the past agonies
Controlling your life
Falling to your knees
Venting your rage

Unleash it
Into the wind
Unleash it
Into the void
Unleash it
Into hell

Acceptance

After Effects

In so much as I can see
There is a shadow over me
My world has stopped turning
My heart and soul are churning
Nothing has remained the same
Ever since that bastard came
But he is welcome to the harlot
A life of misery he has now got
I am still struggling to find
An inner peace in body and mind
People say it will work out
Maybe so, but I still scream and shout

Child Of Pain

Lost and alone
No more have I a home
My family is broken
Bad words have been spoken
Lies rule the day
I wish there was nothing more to say
I am a child of pain

Rejected caresses
Add to life's many stresses
We can overcome
After all has been said and done
Nothing is left sacred
All goodness has been martyred
I am a child of pain

I left myself to blame
While she wanted fame
Society has crumbled asunder
Hark to the anarchists thunder
I have to step up
And refill my cup
I am a child of pain

Disappear

Dead on the inside
No place to hide
This life has beaten me
I am nothing you see

My life is in pieces
My forehead has creases
I want to disappear
Close my ears to not hear

Don't want to experience life
Had enough of the strife
Nothing more to say
Lets call it a day.

Enough!

Do I want her back
No way!
Do I want her love
No way!
Have I had enough
Yes way!
Do I want to move on
Yes Way!

I am done
Done with the lies
I am ready to run
Run as far as I can
Got to get away
Away from her presence
Don't want to hear her say
Say things that mean nothing

Family

There once was a unit
Of people who helped each other
Now it is broken in pieces
My children without their mother

Tears and tantrums every day
Coming from feelings of abandonment
Pain and rejected emotions
Derived from broken sacrament

This is my lot in life
I do it without second thought
I am a parent in every way
The depression I have fought

There is an end in sight
Though sometimes I cannot see
Sticking it out for my children
What will be, will be

Finality

Love is hatred
Love is sin
Do not let her get in

In times of pain
In times of trial
There be no room for self denial

This is life
This is torture
No passions to nurture

I am broken
I am scared
This is how my life has fared

I Wish You Well

Even though you have hurt me
I wish you well
No matter what happens in life
I wish you well
Do not worry about me now 'cos
I wish you well
Never fear my dear
I wish you well

Insomniac Of Rejection

I suffer in my sadness
Plagued with unending madness

Diseased with dead love
Teary rain falls from above

Asinine thoughts in' my head
Tossing and turning in my bed

I am lost for words emotionally
Why did she commit such folly

Never more to share laughter
Now I dream of slaughter

My body is weary and beaten
I huddle alone in my den

A creature of maniac hatred
Suffering the loss of the sacred

Vows that are broken
Lies that are spoken

Take away my comfort
Thus is this twisted man wrought

It Is Over

Stop messing with my head
It seems you want me dead
Out of your way
Forever and a day
I have no place in your life
Though I have made sacrifice
I gave all to you
But now we are through
Why break my heart
Before you did depart
Was my pain not enough
Did you have to be so rough
Of family you know nothing
No respect for wedding ring
My soul you have scarred
My inner self you have marred
But I am strong
And my patience is long
When you fall on your face
I won't help it's not my place
Living with your new man
Who could never love you as I can
Our union is done
You never gave all and had fun
So farewell I will say
With no thought of dismay

Life Marches On

There is no acceptance
Without understanding
There is no understanding
When there is confusion

Love has become ignorance
Hate has taken precedence
This pleasant relationship
Tastes bitter to the lip

I was dead inside
Desperately trying to hide
My torn emotions
Filled with twisted notions

But life marches on
Even when everything is wrong
You pick yourself up
And fill your own cup

In time healing comes
Happiness in your head hums
No more scared and lonely
No more 'if only'

Mother

Mom where are you
I need you
But you have gone now

Mom are you there
I trusted you
But you have betrayed me now

Mom where have you gone
I loved you
But that is over now

Mom I am sad
I miss you
But I will get over it somehow

My Biggest Mistake

For her I would have died
Yet to me she lied
Was the love of my life
My biggest mistake
Oh how I long for a clean break

Walking in this dream
Nothing seems real
My responsibilities on hold
Everything is surreal
Nightmares playing in my head
Filling me with terror
What have I done
Where is my error

How do I fix this broken home
How can I make it right
She is never coming back
Even though she thinks she might
I want nothing from her
This cold selfish girl
The thought of her coming back
Makes me want to hurl

Broken hearts still can bleed
Broken minds still can think
Bleeding terrible thoughts
Into utter despair I sink
People gather around
Some with kindness and compassion
Some to point and laugh
I need to make this decision

Of Emotion And Turmoil

I want to scream
And break down and cry
Had enough of this mess
Just want to fly

When I think it has ended
I realize that it has just begun
I cannot go on like this
Someone has a sick sense of fun

Damn I am so tired
Just want to lay my head down
Give it all up for a while
And wear the misery crown

I wish I was dead inside
So I could not feel this way
No emotions to mess me up
No feelings my moods to sway

I will be alright one day
So they tell me
But right now I suffer
When I should be free

Of Understanding and Acceptance

Wrapped up in her own little world
She sees no-one but herself
And so this story has unfurled
And all is given up for dead

Behold this bringer of sadness
With manic thoughts breeding chaos
A grand lesson in madness
Life's lessons taught well

On her knees begging for more
She gives out her disease
The petulant child becomes the whore
And so the insanity unfolds

Single Forever

I want to be alone
In this state eternal
Better than the moan
Of a faithless partner

There is to much pain
To have a comforting hand
Nothing emotional to gain
Just heartache and sadness

Shattered

Hiding behind my walls
I can see nothing at all
Losing my existence
To painful oblivion

The loss of all I loved
The love I craved
Has shattered me
Making it hard to see

Examine my soul
Dig deep into the hole
That was left behind
There is nothing to find

The clouds are gathering
So I cannot see anything
Still I fight on and on
Even though it be a con

Survivor

The loss of all I loved
The love I craved
Has shattered me
Making it hard to see

Madness leads to sanity
Sanity leads to nothing
Forever forging on
I raise my voice in song

The Hermit

I will hide away
And wait for the day
Stay here in the shadow
With the bitter knowledge I know

Waiting for the end
This heart will never mend
I am cold and aloof
Bitter twisted and uncouth

Bring me the pain
Let me feel again
This nothingness kills me
I wait to be free

The Struggle

What has she done
This fickle temptress
My family has now gone
All for her infidelity

How can I overcome
These depressing moments
Just because she wanted some
My children are motherless

I struggle to clear my head
Fighting anger and pain
Wishing she was dead
Easier than seeing her again

I will get over this
Someday somehow
Find someone else to kiss
And live life again

Time Passes By

Softly softly
This feeling washes over me
Softly softly
The despairing regret

Slowly slowly
It penetrates through
Slowly slowly
Wearing my defences away

Time passes by
And the memory lessons
Moving deeper into subconscious
And I can think again

I can feel
Feel the rising of emotion
I can feel
My body is again awakening

Softly softly
The anger fades away
softly softly
Does the pain recede

Slowly slowly
I can accept this horror
Slowly slowly
I can even understand

Why?

Why she left me?
I cannot say
Maybe she thought
That I was gay
Was I not
Enough of a man?
Or was it just
Because she can
What did I do?
That was so wrong
Maybe she had it planned
All along

Moving On

Fools In Love

Us gentle souls
Compete for love
Needing to fill the holes
In our lonely emotions

Searching High and low
In all the wrong places
Not telling between friend or foe
Gullible and scarred

We are fools in love
Learning hard lessons
Rejected with a shove
Every heartbeat hurts

And then out of the blue
Someone will find you
Someone who is true
Maybe someone like me

Heaven Is!

A family together
A friendship for life
Whatever the weather
No matter the strife

To give love
And be loved in turn
To feel warmth from above
Never a soul to spurn

This is heaven
This place inside
The ability to listen
Never to run and hide

Let The Silence End

Let the silence end
Time to start again my friend
Life is for living
Not for sadness and mourning
The times may be hard
And you may have seen deaths card
But you are alive
This war you will survive
Underneath the hard shell
Your emotions lift and swell
Alive through your pain
Looking for what you will gain
There is always hope
Even when you could not cope
Life rolls on 'til the end
The breaks will mend

Of Life And Enjoyment

Searching for my sanity
I found my life
It was not as it should be
All was in disarray
Lost to the infinity
Struggling with my strife
I was not all that I could be
I have lost my way

And so goes this sad story
Of a life not enjoyed
A tale of utmost woe
Misery and damnation
I never found my glory
I have become soiled
Never letting myself grow
Lost in others insinuation

All hail the enemy
The one who never fights
My best friend for ever
I have let this thing become
Now I search frantically
Never seeing the sights
Going down into the never
Nowhere to hide so I run

Of Life And Emotion

Wandering lost and alone
Never thought I would settle down
Sinking under all this shit
Just trying not to drown
Living life in anticipation
Facing my fears with a frown

This is life dear friend
You have to live with it
So give all you have got
And make the glove fit
Look forward with a smile
And the target you will hit

It is no good to be down
What a waste of your face
With never a smile to give
You look out of place
Cheer up and move on
Regain your lost grace

Of Love And Heartache

Here I sit in a darkened room
Hiding from the light
Cold air chills the room
And tears blur my sight
The opened window behind me
Lets in the night

What possessed you
To cause this pain
What happened to you
That made you insane
Where are you now
Where is your gain

Six months on and I am fine
I can smile again
I have freedom now
No heartache or pain
I close my eyes to the sun
Warmed and feeling sane

What possessed you
To cause this pain
What happened to you
That made you insane
Where are you now
Where is your gain

Of love and heartache
This is the way it goes
Turning us to hate and madness
Thoughts of dark prose
Rhyming in our heads
Where it ends heaven only knows

Soul In Obscurity

See the mist
Rolling in over the hills
Crawling ever closer
Out in the moonlight it spills

I feel so lost
My soul is in obscurity
I am paying the cost
For another's mistakes
Bare feet cold in the frost
I wander aimlessly

The mist brings blindness
A blurring of my vision
This cancerous rejection
cannot be removed by incision

Behold the light
Leading me onwards
Never trusting my sight
I stumble and fall
On my knees ready to fight
The light fades away

Hiding in the murk
I try to find my path
Searching in the crevasse
I discover naught but wrath

Sunken

The depression of my mind
Is my greatest enemy
Fear of what's left behind
Eats me away slowly

I am sinking deep
Into this madness
My sanity I try keep
I get lost in my sadness

Inferior feelings fill me
Burning all emotions away
This is me I can see
Living in night not day

Hating my very thoughts
Searching for myself
Completely out of sorts
I am hidden on the shelf

Understanding

All she ever wanted
Is now in her grasp
All she ever needed
She left behind

I am alright now
I am starting to get it
The why, the when, the how
It is all coming back

Not mature enough
To be with her family
Thinking life was tough
So she ran away

I am better off today
Without her problems
Her sullen face gone away
I can see again

Valentines

Valentines
Oh bloody valentines
Cupid the stupid
Shot the wrong girl
Now life is bad

This is all for now
Nothing left to say
Bright new beginnings
A whole lot more torment
Now life is bad

Not The End

Dry your eyes
Begone tears of sadness
This is not the end
But the start of future gladness

I know it is hard
And you cannot see ahead
But memories linger on
When all has been said

You do not have to walk alone
Friends and family gather round
Through the grieving
Laughter is a precious sound

The absent one reappears
In your child's eyes
In the innocent smile
That happens when time flies

The pain will lessen
Be overtaken with joy
Life does go on
Do not your life destroy

Oblivion

One more cigarette before I am dead
To clear the voices in my head
Celebrating my pain with another drink
Not allowing my brain space to think
Ignorant in my own oblivion
No thoughts to ponder on
Escape comes so cheap
All rolled up so neat
This is not the answer my friend
It will catch up to you in the end

Of Love And Dissemination

Love is a fantasy
Driven by mankind's need
Lost in lies of passion
And the will to disperse our seed

Emotions spread their legs
For the next through the door
Looking in all the wrong places
Becoming a dirty cheap whore

We believe our own lies
Following the voice in our head
Listening to the unreal
All our passions are dead

Blindly stumbling on
Through life's great masquerade
Following the nearest fool
On this grand insipid parade

Yet still we search
Never will we find our place
Apathetic and numb
We have fallen from grace

Of Love And Friendship

I was lonely and she found me
She took me in and gave me comfort
Built me up and let me stand
Gave me strength to deal with hurt

Forever grateful will I be
She is my good friend for eternity
I wish her all the best in life
For she deserves it all you see

She is the lady of the dream
Beautiful and shining radiance
She needs to know for certain
That this was not mischance

All her love will return to her
Come raining down all around
Filling her with peace and desire
A new happiness will be found

3 years on

Empty Promises

I frown upon your ignorance
After-all you are a mother
Your children wanted your acceptance
Not to be raised by another

This perpetual curse in motion
Dark words hissed out loud
Darker the deeds by your hand
That make me feel alone in a crowd

I curse the ground you walk upon
I curse the air that gives you life
May your days be long and plenty
So you have a full measure of strife

May happiness always be fleeting
May you never settle for anything

Wait . . . . I retract my words
You already do this to yourself

Narrow Path

Black as midnight
This nocturnal mood
Arising from depths untapped
And inspiring me to brood

Taking me away from my life
It leads me down a narrow path
'Til I am lost in my head
Leaving my kin to deal with the aftermath

Of Past and Present

It felt so good when we were together
Sadly that is when the pain comes
Falling fast into the ever reaching nether
The god of sadness a guitar softly strums

We suffer alone
Silent as stone
Warm like bone
Live to atone

Past memories now dragged out into sunlight
Scarring and burning under smiling skies
Driven to pain for the sake of doing right
Forgive me when this empty shell cries

This my creed
No more greed
Dying I plead
Never to breed

In the halls of madness unrelenting
I take a bow and find my true place
My head bent low to receive the blessing
From the dark god I see in your face